Pack a Sweater

Preparing Boomers For Long Term Care

Author: Wallace R. Nichols, J.D., M.B.A.

Preface

This book is because of Paige, who has enabled me in many ways to help my family, and in doing so, provide guidance, assistance, and instruction to many other families along the way.

This work is for my family, nuclear and extended, but especially for my children, Ashlea and Jarod, who have never lost faith in me. I've learned so much about how to best serve the needs of certain niches of the American consuming public by learning how to best protect my family.

This effort is dedicated to all my clients along the way, past and future, who have and will decided to take the journey with me.

Specifically though, this edition is intended as a tribute of sorts to Johnny R. Ballard, who like me, most clearly saw this vision in terms of how to best protect and help his own family, yet, in doing so, intuitively also saw this path as the same path to healing, growth and becoming the best he could be, with what time we have left.

With Dad, Barb, and Jeff in mind...

eBook ISBN 9780988295018

Paperback ISBN 9780988295025

Contents

Introduction.......7

PART I:.......13

I'm a Statistic.......15

The Toll on Family Caregivers.......27

Incapacity Can Come At Any Age.......43

Why I'm Telling You This Story.......57

Perceptions of Long-Term Care Costs.......61

The Facts About Long-Term Care.......67

MetLife Market Survey of Long-Term Care Costs 2012.......71

Genworth Cost of Care Survey 2014.......85

Comparison and Conclusion as to the MetLife and Genworth Reports.......88

Carriers Leaving the LTCi Arena.......90

Individual Participation in the LTCi Marketplace.......92

PART II.......99

What Is Long-Term Care Planning?.......101

Medicaid Planning at the State Level—Focus: Georgia.......111

Paying for LTC—The LTC Timeline and Insurance.......121

Self-Funding LTC Expenses.......125

Basic Planning for Everyone 141

Ancillary Documents 147

The Last Will & Testament 148

Advanced Planning Techniques 151

A Hypothetical Illustration 155

Crisis Planning 167

VA Aid & Attendance Planning 189

Conclusions 205

APPENDIX 209

Table 1 210

Table 2 211

About the Author 217

Introduction

I appreciate so much you sharing with me your interests in exploring one of this generation's most complex and challenging issues. The issues underlying long-term care planning and incapacity planning are among the most pronounced issues of our time. I say this with confidence because, for the last 3 to 5 years, 10,000 people *per day* have reached the age of 65 years. This trend will continue for the next 5 to 10 years, until the baby boomer generation has become entirely elderly—in the year 2030.

Before we delve directly into the technical details underlying the major themes here, I want to give you a short roadmap. The first macro-level is to define and discuss the problem(s) we are confronting in terms of the longevity crisis. I'll start by telling you about how I got involved in this line of work as a focus of my law practice. I'll discuss why what seems like the most desirable way to age, in-place, can be anything but, unless one chooses to overlook the impact on one's family members. Next, I'll discuss incapacity preparedness issues. We'll get into long-term care facts, from three perspectives: nationally, Georgia statewide, and in the Atlanta metropolitan area.

So as not to leave you in a state of despair, up the creek and without a paddle as they say, we'll transition to a search for solutions via the planning process. We'll discuss the analytical approach that is long-term care planning.

The discussion then turns to Medicaid law. We'll look at paying for long-term care, the aging timeline and how insurance has impacted it and vice-versa. Then, I'll go to the heart of the matter and speak of asset protection approach to LTC issues via Medicaid planning. Then, we'll pull back a little and review some basic planning techniques, so that you understand the advanced strategies that become Medicaid Asset Protection Planning.

For the not-faint of heart daredevils of this generation whose motto has always been and yet remains, "Live for Today," I've included a chapter on crisis planning to cover the cowboy way. Then, an overview of VA Aid and Attendance Pension Benefit Planning for war-time veterans or their surviving spouses. Then, we'll get into long-term care and estate planning and asset transfer strategies. That will bring us to the conclusion and my heart-felt thanks for taking this journey through the looking glass with me and a call to action to engage the stark reality that confronts our generation: outliving our money and doing something about it!

PART I:
THE PROBLEM(s)

1

I'm a Statistic

Let's start with my family as an empirical example. I was born at the tail-end of the Baby Boom Generation, in 1959. Conversely, my siblings were born at the height of the baby-boom generation (my sister born in 1947 and my brother born in 1949). My parents were Depression Era Babies, each born in 1930. In my father's generation, the big scare was nuclear war or dying of a heart attack. For my older siblings, although the threat of nuclear holocaust loomed over their heads during their formative years, medical technology advanced to the point that heart attacks no longer remained the focal point of concern. Indeed, even my father's generation saw heart attacks relegated to a lesser concern as compared with cancer. For those Depression-Era Babies who were fortunate enough to live past age 65, they even witnessed cancer succumbing to the ever increasing technological capabilities of modern medical science in many instances. So for all the wonders that medical science has provided us, do you think my father or many in his generation recognized the problems that these technological advancements were leaving us? Do you think that my older siblings or many in their generation recognized the corresponding financial issues related to longevity? Well, the answer to the former question is clearly, "no," while the answer to the latter is "not really."

My father's generation was concerned with dying prematurely. Accordingly, his generation focused their financial planning primarily on life insurance. I call that type of planning a "Bet-to-Die Strategy." You see, when my dad was growing up, most people were dead by the age of 65. So he never planned on living past 65. Accordingly, all of his life insurance strategy was designed for him to expire before age 65, in which case he won the bet with the insurance company. If he lived past age 65, he was still alive, but he lost his bet with the insurance company. From a financial planning standpoint, the insurance company won the bet. Understand that my dad never really understood life insurance, therefore he never really trusted the insurance companies. As a result, he bought the cheapest insurance on his life that he could -- term life insurance. When he didn't purchase term life insurance, he purchased universal life policies back in the 1980s, and those policies ended up chewing up any cash values that remained inside of them as he aged. By the time my dad reached his mid-to-late 70s, he began to change his strategy to what I'll call, a "pay-as-you-go strategy." He began purchasing annuities in accord with professional advice (not mine of course). Annuities are great devices to use generally, but not the types of annuities he was sold at that age. So once again, my dad fell into the trap of conventional thinking: making the type of return on investment sufficient to grow money under the status quo. As we shall see, and as is the focus of this book, the type of planning required to deal with the challenges of our time is a little different - - almost 180° different. But, I digress. Everything ticked along nicely and my dad turned 79 years old in 2009 with a chipper attitude towards life and a healthy bank account, his

own home free and clear and two brand-new vehicles. Here's a picture of my mom and dad that year. Scarcely a year after this image was taken, my father fell victim to a massive hemorrhagic stroke that required him to be immediately institutionalized and he has since remained institutionalized.

My brother is a Vietnam War veteran. He served in Vietnam during the worst of the worst periods. He shipped out to Saigon in December, 1967 and landed there in January 1968, just in time for the worst Tet Offensive of the war's history. After surviving his tour of duty there, he returned stateside in the spring of 1969. He received an honorable discharge in 1969, and returned to civilian life in the small town of Hobbs where we were living. After working for years in the oil fields doing manual labor, my brother began experiencing multiple health issues, ultimately qualifying for Agent Orange disability benefits as he reached middle-age. It goes without saying that the Agent Orange exposure stemmed from his tour of duty in Vietnam. After my brother got into his early 60s, he developed cancer. He was diagnosed with both lung and throat cancer.

The marvels of medical science have extended his life for several years. However, at the end of his cancer treatments, he required assistance for many activities of daily living ("ADL"). This type of life became his reality for the next six years. As of the writing of this book, my brother has reported to me that the doctors have told him that there is little more they can do to extend his life and thus, he is in the final stages of his life. Nonetheless, my brother has required assistance with his ADLs for over six years. Unfortunately, this is not a unique experience for members of this generation.

The hidden lesson here is this: for the first time in American history, we are living in an age where multiple generations of a family may require long-term care assistance at the same time. Now, do you think that either my father or my brother ever contemplated that they would both be incapacitated at the same time? Of course they didn't! They both believed that each would predecease the other. My father always planned to die before any of his children; that's the normal progress of life. My brother, being a child of the 60s, thought that he would either: a) be killed in action in Vietnam and never return; or, b) predecease my father as a result of his lifestyle choices. Again, both of these men were using a "bet-to-die strategy," and neither of them ever contemplated simply being incapacitated and unable to perform ADLs without assistance.

This was the fallacy of using the conventional wisdom of their day. No one contemplated the impacts that modern science would have upon absolutely every aspect of our lives, from personal computers, to microwave ovens, to chemicals that could create cancers to ravage our bodies, to chemicals that could help stop the ravaging of our bodies that were caused by the other chemicals! So, you can see how using the wrong strategy can prove to be financially debilitating. But it also has an intangible cost that neither of them were actually contemplating: the emotional toll and opportunity costs that it takes upon those around them, mostly family members, and especially the ones we haven't discussed yet - the female family members.

2

The Toll on Family Caregivers

After my father had fallen victim to the stroke, my mother was forced to quickly come up to speed in terms of handling all the tasks and decision-making that she had previously delegated to my father. As she was the same age as he, this sudden change took quite a burden on her in many ways. Naturally, sudden change brings along with it an increased stress level. Increased stress takes a toll on one's health. My father stayed in intensive care at the regional Hospital for several weeks. Then he was moved to a regular room in the same hospital. As we'll discuss later in this work, Medicare only pays costs for 100 days. My father's hospitalization and impending rehabilitation was using up those days very quickly!

My father's health improved to the point of where he no longer required hospitalization. But that didn't mean he could go home. Neither did it mean he didn't require substantial rehabilitation services as well as assistance with his ADLs and bodily functions. For those, my father required admission into a long-term care facility. Now my mother was forced to negotiate a contract with the long-term care facility, otherwise known as a nursing home. These contracts are very complex, even for a lawyer. To make matters worse, my mother was feeling like she was in a "take it or leave it" position. Not only was my mother not accustomed to making decisions of this magnitude alone, she was still not over the fact that this calamity had even occurred to my father! She was not sufficiently emotionally stable to make any types of decisions of really any magnitude, let alone analytical enough to make decisions like these, which involved complex matters, health care concerns, and long-term drains on both cash flow and total resources. Despite the support my siblings and I offered my mother, she was determined to make these important decisions on her own. What we witnessed was my mother vacillating from one extreme to the other. She was making wildly emotional decisions that were not based on logic or in consideration of long-term consequences. She certainly had no background in Medicare or Medicaid law, which is complex enough on its own, notwithstanding all the other factors involved in these decision-making processes. In short, she ended up making far less than optimal decisions. Naturally, all of this had a detrimental impact on her long-term financial stability. But what we didn't see was the impact that this situation was having on her health.

Within about 3 to 4 months of my father's stroke, my mother's blood pressure was so dramatically high that it caused her to suffer from some mild cardio arrhythmia, just shy of a heart attack. Next, it turns out that she has a bleeding ulcer. So, my mother had to be hospitalized. Now we had my father in one long-term care facility and my mother hospitalized in another facility.

What I haven't told you so far is that my parents live in a very rural area of West Texas. As a matter of fact, the little town in which they reside, Eldorado, is about 50 miles from the local regional hospital. The regional hospital is located in San Angelo, Texas. So, my parents' property, both real and personal, was located an hour away from either of them and both of them were housed in institutions. I live 1,500 miles away from them. My brother was incapacitated and couldn't travel to their town at that time to be of any consequential assistance. My sister lives in the Houston metropolitan area a day's drive away. Chaos was knocking at the door.

My older sister has been a flight attendant since 1983. For the last decade or so, she's been working international flights. Of course, she was on the opposite side of the planet when these events were transpiring; Murphy's Law reigned supreme. As the oldest female child, it seems that our national cultural norms dictated that she should be the one to drop her life and moved to take care of our parents. Fortunately, since she works for a major airline, she had available to her the benefits of the Family Medical Leave Act. But this is not paid time off; this is merely time off without penalty of being discharged. She still would suffer the financial consequences of not being able to work. Of course she could use her paid vacation benefits, but those only last so long. And, it is not really fair to ask someone to use their hard-earned vacation benefits simply to take care of family matters. I'm sure you would agree that at this point the situation had turned into quite the debacle. Fortunately, our mother encountered a stroke of good fortune in terms of good health. Because she had taken quite good care of herself over the years, my mother recovered very quickly and was able to return to her "new normal" and resume taking care of dad.

Let's review the situation objectively at this point. Two generations of the males of the family had become incapacitated. As a direct consequence, the two oldest females in the family were then placed in highly stressful situations. The increased stress had a detrimental impact on the health and the financial stability of the elder female, and threatened the financial livelihood and an unplanned relocation of the other. The "bet-to-die" strategy was not working well for any member of the family. In fact, it was wreaking havoc on everyone's lives. As we will see later, the statistical probability is very high that there will be a detrimental impact on the health of the older female members of the family when this type of scenario develops.

As life goes, my family wasn't out of the woods yet. At that time, my dad required extensive rehabilitation services, and those services were costing in the neighborhood of $11,000 per month. Being very private about their financial situation, my mother was unwilling to discuss their position with any of us. Since they had just purchased a brand-new pickup for my father, I immediately suggested that perhaps the new pickup should be disposed of and the cash proceeds used to offset these new expenses. That idea flew like a brick. What everyone knew, but my mother refused to admit, was that she was depleting my parent's liquid assets very quickly. Moreover, my mother was now having to commute 45 miles each way, each day, to spend time with my father and monitor his progress. His physical progress was somewhat good, but his mental progress was more variable. On other days, this situation reversed. Eventually, my father's physical progress improved to the point where he could move to the smaller, less resourced facility in the little town in which they live. Being around more familiar faces, my father's mental wherewithal began to return to him a little faster.

Alas, my mother soon developed back problems that required surgery. She had been suffering back pain for a long time and suddenly become unbearable. So, once again, we were faced with my mom being 45 miles away in the larger town where the hospital was located, and my father being in the little town in the long-term care facility and no one around to manage their assets. Nobody was close by to make health care decisions for them, in the event that

such decisions needed to be made. My dad was not fully mentally competent to make decisions of any significant gravity. My mother was going to be under the knife, so she was going to be incapacitated for at least a short period of time. We had no choice.
My sister and I both took time off work and flew to be with our parents, while our mother recovered from her surgery.

Our mother convalesced for a month following her surgery. We had to have her placed in a Medicare bed at the small hospital facility there in that little town, and then moved her into a "hotel-type" arrangement at the same long-term care facility where my father was residing—by now back in Eldorado. Obviously, my sister had to apply for family medical leave benefits, and I had to do my best to practice law and run the other aspects of my life from a laptop computer on the Internet. At this point, it became pretty obvious that a new estate plan had been put in place. So I began to do what I do to resolve that end of the situation - at least as fast as our mother would allow me to do so.

Once again, my sister felt the societal pressure to place her life on hold and move to where my parents live to take care of my mother. So, my sister had to go back to Houston and finish up the one last flight that she had already had scheduled, as it was too late for her employer to replace her on that flight with such short notice, until her medical leave papers went through. Meanwhile, as she was preparing the house in which she lived for sale, she slipped and broke her foot.

At this point, I trust that you can see a cycle repeating itself. Older people dealing with stressful situations involving loss of health, financial resources, and making major lifestyle changes suffer a toll on their physical well-being. In our society, these pressures generally fall on the spouse of the incapacitated or the oldest female child of the family. Consequently, the incapacitation of one family member often results in the diminished lifestyles of not only themselves, but the spouse and their oldest adult child, who frequently turns out to be female.

3

Incapacity Can Come At Any Age

Incapacity is not reserved merely for the aged though. Paige, my wife, was a beautiful, young, successful businesswoman in the prime of her life. At age 41 she was diagnosed with Stage III colon and kidney cancer. She had to drop the business that she was running, the house that she had built and was moving into, and undergo immediate surgery. It took roughly 6 months to a year for her to return to some semblance of "normal" with respect to her life pre-diagnosis.

Disability happens more often than you'd imagine. The Counsel for Disability Awareness data show that just over one in four of today's 20-year-olds will become disabled before they die. Over 37 million Americans are classified as disabled; about 12% of the total population. More than half of those disabled Americans are in the working years from 18 to 64 years of age. Over 5% of US workers, about 8.8 million people, were receiving Social Security Disability ("SSDI") benefits at the end of 2012. In December 2012, there were over 2 1/2 million disabled workers in their 20s, 30s, and 40s receiving SSDI benefits. The chances of becoming disabled is fairly staggering according to the Council for Disability Awareness Personal Disability Quotient Calculator (respectively, "CDA" and "PDQ"). The following statistics come from the CDA's PDQ disability risk calculator:

A typical female, age 35, 5'4", 125 pounds, non-smoker, who works mostly an office job, with some outdoor physical responsibilities, and who leads a healthy lifestyle has the following risks:

- 24% chance of becoming disabled for 3 months or longer during her working career;
    - With a 38% chance that the disability would last 5 years or longer;
    - And with the average disability of someone like her lasting 82 months.
- A typical male, age 35, 5'10", 170 pounds, non-smoker, who works in an office job, with some outdoor physical responsibilities, and who leads a healthy lifestyle has the following risk:
    - 21% chance of becoming disabled for 3 months or

longer during his working career;

- With a 38% chance that the disability would last 5 years longer,
- And with the average disability for someone like him lasting 82 months.

- If the same person used tobacco and weigh 210 pounds the risk would increase to a 45% chance of becoming disabled for 3 months or longer.

A sample of factors that increase the risk of disability are the following:

excess body weight, tobacco use, high risk activities or behaviors, chronic conditions such as: diabetes, high blood pressure, back pain, anxiety or depression, frequent alcohol consumption or substance abuse.

A sample of factors that decrease the risk of disability are as follows: maintaining a healthy body weight, no tobacco use, healthy diet and sleep habits, regular exercise, moderate no alcohol consumption, avoidance of high-risk behaviors including substance abuse, maintaining a healthy stress level, and effective treatment of chronic health conditions.

To calculate your own personal disability quotient (PDQ), go to: http://www.whatsmyPDQ.org. The data show that working Americans greatly underestimate the risk of disability. The US Social Security Administration fact sheet February 7, 2013 data shows 64% of workers believe that they have a 2% or less chance of being disabled for 3 months or more during their working career. The actual odds for a worker entering the workforce today are about 25%. Most working Americans estimate that their own chances of experiencing a long-term disability are substantially lower than the average workers according to the Council for disability awareness, disability divide consumer disability awareness study, 2010.

According to a study performed by Christopher Tarver Robertson, Richard Egelhof, and Michael Hoke published August 8, 2008 titled "Get Sick, Get Out: The Medical Causes Of Home Mortgage Foreclosures," medical problems contributed to half of all home foreclosure filings in 2006. According to bankruptcy statistics published by US courts the 12 month period ending December 2007, in the American Journal of Medicine, June 4, 2009, "Medical Bankruptcy in the United

States 2007," medical problems contributed to 62% of all personal bankruptcies filed in the United States in 2007, an increase of over 500,000. This is up 50% from the results from a similar 2001 study. According to the CDA's 2013 long-term disability claims review, the following were leading causes of new disability claims in 2012:

- Musculoskeletal/connective tissue disorders 28 1/2%;
- Cancer 14.6%;
- Injuries and poisoning 10.6%;
- Mental disorders 8.9%;
- Cardiovascular/circulatory disorders 8.2%.

According to the Social Security Administration reports for 2012 and

2013, 65% of initial SSDI claim applications were denied in 2012. The average monthly benefit paid by Social Security Disability Insurance or SSDI at the end of 2012 was only $1,130. The average SSDI payment for males was $1,256 per month while the average SSDI monthly benefit for females was $993. Less than 5% of disabling accidents and illnesses are work-related. The other 95% are not, meaning that Workers Compensation doesn't cover them, according to “Long-Term Disability Claims Review, 2012,” published by the CDA.

Given our active lifestyles, genetics, polluted environment, and often poor dietary selections and lifestyle choices, incapacity can strike at any age. In fact, most of the "right to die" cases have involved young females ages 18 to 35 who are stricken down in the primes of their lives. Who should make the appropriate healthcare decisions when such a young person is incapacitated? Such a person is an emancipated adult. Therefore, their parents have no automatic legal standing to make such decisions. Who is to make the decisions regarding the care of any children for whom a young person might be responsible? Absent guidance put in place by the child's parents, the court is left to a hearing process to make findings of fact to determine who should be the child's legal guardian until emancipation, in such a case with a parent is no longer available to make such decisions. That means that someone other than a person whom the parent truly knew was appropriate to raise the child may end up raising the child, simply because another person was able to convince the court that they were the more appropriate person, regardless of who the parent actually would have chosen. What kind of plan is in place to ensure that any business enterprise which such young person may be running continues to be a going concern in their absence? Employees of such a business may be left entirely without legal authority to make decisions necessary to keep the business afloat while the owner is incapacitated. Co-owners or family members may be left to resort to litigation to determine the appropriate ownership and transference of not only business decision-making authority, the business ownership. A Will, or a "Plan-to-Die" strategy addresses none of these issues; a "Plan to Live" strategy does.

4

Why I'm Telling You This Story

Because of the wonders that modern technology has brought us, the Internet, enhanced communication devices, portability, the ability to access information and contact people from anywhere on the planet at almost any time, my family developed a solution that ultimately avoided much of this calamity of lifestyles and failure to create and implement a "Plan-to-Live" strategy. However, it was very expensive and very stressful and involved the expenditure of a significant sum of resources before the problem was ultimately resolved in a positive fashion.

That's the purpose of this book: to show you that you do not have to go through the same situation with your family. You can remedy the bulk of these horrific decisions by simply implementing proper planning now. You probably aren't going to die; you're probably going to live—too long!
You have to buy insurance when you don't need the benefits. You have to transfer assets before

creditors get a claim against you or they can undo the transfers to pay themselves. You have to anticipate the icebergs in the ocean with more than one contingency plan—have a thick hull, numerous water-tight bulkheads, PLUS plenty of lifeboats.

Most of what my mother was frantically doing before she agreed to engage in such planning with my sister and I was tantamount to merely rearranging chairs on the deck of the Titanic after it hit the iceberg. But if one doesn't even have a plan and, like the proverbial ostrich with its head in the sand, is simply ignoring the probabilities, then that person is more akin to the owners of the Titanic who failed to provide sufficient lifeboats for the Titanic—tragically and catastrophically myopic, uncaring, and irresponsible.

5

Perceptions of Long-Term Care Costs

I recently conducted a survey of selected individuals from the Metropolitan Atlanta area and asked them a variety of questions to test their collective knowledge about long-term care in Georgia. I think you'll find their answers interesting. Further, I think that the average of these answers over the period of time, and the number of people to which I asked them, provide a fairly accurate statistical measurement of the average knowledge of the general population in the northern Metropolitan Atlanta, Georgia area in these particular topics. The average responses to each of the questions asked are as follows, respectively:

- **What do you think the average cost per month is for skilled nursing facilities ("SNFs") in Georgia?** 19% thought the range would lie between $1,501-$2,500; 31% believed that the range lay between $2,501-$3,500; 31% believed the range lay between $3,501-$4,500; and 19% believed the cost was $5,501 or greater.

- **What do you think the average cost per month is for assisted living facilities ("ALCs") in Georgia?** 7% believed those costs lay between $1,501-$2,500; 40% believed the cost range lay between $2,501 and $3,500; 40% believed the cost lay between $3,501-$4,500; and 13% believed the costs were $4,501 or greater.
- **How much do you think the average hourly rate is for in-home service providers in Georgia?** 14% believed the hourly range was $6-$12 per hour; 71% believe the cost was

$19-$21 per hour; and 14% believed the cost was $35-$50 per hour.

- **How much is your net worth?** 44% of those surveyed claimed net worth of up to $250,000; 25% claimed a net worth of $251,000-$500,000; 13% claimed a net worth of $501,000-$1 million; and 19% claimed a net worth of $1 million or greater.
- **Do you or someone in your immediate family have Alzheimer's?** 27% of respondents said "Yes"; 73% said "No".
- **How long do you think the average length of stay in a**

long-term care ("LTC") facility is? 33% said 0 to 2 years; 20% said 2 to 3 years; 47% said 3+ years.

You should stop now, ask yourself these same questions, jot down your answers to each, and then compare them to what you discover in the next chapter.

6

The Facts About Long-Term Care

First, we'll look at 2012 data compiled and reported by MetLife, one of the nation's leading insurance provider for LTCi. Next, we'll look at 2014 data reported Genworth, another of the nation's leading LTCi carriers. MetLife reported mean average statistics, while Genworth reported median average statistics. This is a great way of comparing all the data to determine where the most probable "true" middle range lies, in terms of "actual" or "expected" costs any random consumer might pay. First, let me take you down a brief (and hopefully painless) detour of statistical terminology so that I ensure you understand the significance and reliability of these reports.

A *mean* average is the total of all observations divided by the number of those observations. A *median* is the exact middle point value of all reported observations. A mean average is a statistically viable method of smoothing all reported values in the search for a value one might expect to observe in the "long run" or "on the average" for a large number of observations. A mean can be highly sensitive given a distribution of only a few observations, or data points. Thus, an extreme on either the high or low side of reported observations can skew a mean average, sometimes drastically. On the other hand, a median data point shows the exact middle of a distribution, where half of the observed values lie above that value, and half below. Thus, a median is robust against extreme values in the small-sample size study. As the sample size increases to larger sizes, we would expect the median to approximate the mean. Accordingly, a look at both reports, one based on 2012 mean averages and one based on 2014 medians, we can get closer to a revelation of the most-likely expected consumer costs of long-term care and a more accurate concept of the annual growth rate ("AGR") of LTC costs. So, somewhere in the morass of evidence lies the "truth." Our job is to ferret it out. Our quest: to determine the expected costs of long-term care so we can properly plan to meet it. Now, let's return to the reports and enhance our understanding.

MetLife Market Survey of Long-Term Care Costs 2012

According to the most recent MetLife Market Survey of Long-Term Care Costs 2012, the average nursing home stay duration is two years and five months. This figure is the current *mean* average. With many long-term illnesses, the stay can be much longer. The late President Ronald Reagan lived for 10 years after his diagnosis of Alzheimer's disease. The mean average assisted living stays are about 2 1/2 years also. So, the expenditures once a person is no longer able to be completely self-sufficient run roughly 4 to 5 years. On average, the outlays will be lesser initially, gradually increasing over time.

The mean average cost of care in the United States for a SNF stay in 2012 was $90,520 for private room. MetLife 2012 Market Survey of Long-Term Care Costs. That translated to $248 per day. For semi-private room, the cost is $81,030 per year. *Id.* That cost translated to a mean average per day cost of $222. For an Alzheimer's patient, the cost averaged as high as $95,265 per year. That averages $261 per day. It is noteworthy that 80% of all SNFs surveyed charge the same rate whether or not the patient was afflicted with Alzheimer's.

Accordingly, the statistics given are for those that charge differently for Alzheimer's, e.g., patients requiring monitors, security/alarmed doors, locked units, or separate wings. Assisted living centers (ALC's) who also provided care for Alzheimer's patients with perhaps less severe symptoms, charged $83,950 per year, or $230 per day. It is equally noteworthy that 72% of all ALC's surveyed charge the same rate whether or not the patient was diagnosed with Alzheimer's. Again, the statistics given are for those facilities that charge differently for Alzheimer's patients: those requiring monitors, security/alarmed doors, locked units, or separate wings.

As you can see, the 2012 average cost of SNF care nationwide, including Alzheimer's patients, **averaged over $7,000 per month!** Now, this statistic is somewhat influenced by the more costly care required to properly care for Alzheimer's patients. Alzheimer's is growing at an alarming rate. Alzheimer's increased by 46.1% as a cause of death between 2000 and 2006, while causes of death from prostate cancer, breast cancer, heart disease, and HIV, all declined during that same time period. Every 70 seconds, someone in America develops Alzheimer's. By midcentury, someone will develop Alzheimer's every 33 seconds. Currently, one in eight people over age 65 has Alzheimer's disease. In 2010, the Alzheimer's Association published a report titled, "Alzheimer's Disease Facts and Figures," that explore different types of dementia, causes and risk factors, and the cost involved providing health care, among other areas. In addition to these statistics, this report provided the following eye opening statistics:

- An estimated 5.3 million Americans of all ages have Alzheimer's disease. This figure includes 5.1 million people age 65 and older and 200,000 individuals under age 65 to have younger onset Alzheimer's.

- The number of people age 65 and older with Alzheimer's disease is expected to reach 7.7 million in 2030 - more than a 50% increase from the 5.1 million age 65 and older currently affected.
- By 2050, the number of individuals age 65 and older with Alzheimer's is projected to number between 11 million and 16 million - unless medical breakthroughs identifies ways to prevent or more effectively treat the

disease.

Clearly, Alzheimer's is a major factor driving both current costs, and projected costs, of long-term care in the United States.

Excluding the Alzheimer's statistics, the 2012 mean average cost of a SNF nationwide was close to $7,000 per month. Services provided at nursing homes typically include the following:

- room and board;
- nursing care;
- medication management;
- personal care (assistance with ADLs); and
- Social and recreational

activities.

"Basic" services at ALC's averaged $40,104 per year, or $3,342 per month in 2012. *Id.* Some examples of additional services provided add to the costs as follows:

- assistance with bathing - $181;
- assistance with dressing - $236;
- assistance with other services (e.g., toilet, eating, continence care) $504;
- assistance with medication administration - $347.

The mean average cost of home healthcare in the United States in

2012 averaged between 17 and $21 per hour. So, even if a person needed only part-time care (that would mean 1040 hours per year, as there are 2080 work hours in a "normal" work year), the cost would be $20,800, on the average. If a person will need full-time assistance, yet wanted to remain aging in-home, the cost would be at least $39,520 per year. Thus, in-home care, if possible, is not much cheaper than either a SNF or an ALC.

Now, let's bring this down to the state level: here, I'll use Georgia. The mean average cost for SNF care in Georgia broke down as follows in

2012: semi private - $5,688; private $6,915. By ZIP Code, this breaks down as follows, for ZIP Codes in Atlanta beginning with 303, the **low** was $160 per day, with a high of $350, an average of $218 per day. In the Marietta area, ZIP Codes beginning in 300, per day rate was $140, the high $217, averaging $181 per day. For the remainder of the state, the semi-private per day rate have a low of $130, and a high of $233, averaging $162 per day for semi-private room. The same measurements for a private room are as follows, Atlanta: low $160 per day, high $450 per day, average $250 per day. In the Marietta ZIP Codes (300), the lowest private room was $165 per day, a high $305, averaging $262 per day. The rest of the state fell out as follows for private room: low $135, high $246, average $170 per day.

The 2012 rates for ALCs in Georgia averaged a base rate of $3,077 per month. These data breakdown as follows for Atlanta ZIP Codes beginning in 303, the low rate was $1,500 per month and the high was $4,095 per month, yielding an average per month cost of $3,090. For Alpharetta ZIP Codes beginning and 300, the low was $1,800 per month, the high $3,760, yielding an average of $2,952 per month. The remaining areas of the state had a low of $2,350 per month, a high of $3,900, yielding an average of $3,188 per month.

The average cost in Georgia for per-hour home healthcare services functioning as a Home Health Aide in 2012, was $19 per hour. For Atlanta's ZIP Codes beginning in 303, the, the low $15, the high $21, yielding an average hourly rate of $18. For Marietta ZIP Codes ending in 300, the low was $15, the high $19, yielding an average per hour rate of $17. For the rest of the state, the low was $15 per hour, the high $24, yielding an average of $19.50 per hour. For those workers functioning as a homemaker or companion, the rates in the Atlanta ZIP Codes beginning at 303 had a low of $15 per hour, a high of $19, averaging $17 per hour. Those in the Marietta ZIP Codes beginning and 300, had a low of $15, a high of $19, averaging $18 per hour. For the rest of the state, homemaker services have a low of $15 per hour, a high of $21 per hour, averaging $18 per hour. Homemakers or companions provide services that include light housekeeping, meal preparation, transportation, and companionship. This type of care is often appropriate for those with Alzheimer's disease or other forms of dementia who may be physically healthy, but require supervision.

Homemakers and companions are not trained to provide hands-on assistance with ADLs such as bathing and dressing. In sum then, home health care in Georgia average in 2012 was about $18 per hour. So, it roughly approximated the national average: $18,720 for halftime service, and $37,440 per year for full-time services. Overall then, the *mean* average monthly cost LTC in Georgia in 2012 was $6,302 for SNF's, $3,077 for ALC's (base rate), $1,517 to $3,033+ for a Home Health Aide, and $1,473 to $2,947 per month for a Homemaker/companion.

Genworth Cost of Care Survey 2014
Now, the Genworth Cost of Care Survey 2014 study reports the median cost of care nationally to be $87,600 for a private room. That's $240 per day, or $7,300 per month. Genworth calculated a five-year annual growth rate ("AGR") of 4.19%. The national median 2014 price of a semi-private room was $77,380, or $212/day--$6,448 per month. The five-year AGR was 3.91%. The national median costs for Assisted Living Facilities ("ALFs") in 2014 were $42,000 annually, or $3,500 per month. The five-year AGR was 4.29%. Nationally, at-home care assistance ranged from $19-$20 per hour for Home Health

Care. The median wage for a home Health Aide was $20/hour yielding a five-year AGR of 1.32%. The national median price for a homemaker/companion was $19/hour, showing a five-year AGR of 1.20%. The median price for Adult Day Health Care ("ADC") was $65/day which annualizes to $16,900, or $1,408/month. ADC has a five-year AGR of 3.4%. Drilled down to the state level, the Genworth 2014 report for Georgia shows a median cost of $192/day for a private room SNF, which equates to $5,825/month, or $69,898 per year. A semi-private room in a SNF was $5,475 per month, or $65,700 annually for

2014. Both these categories ranged from a low daily rate of $116 to a high of $240 for semi-private and $271 per day for private room. These categories both shared a 3% AGR.

ALFs in Georgia showed a median base rate of $2,500 for 2014 with an AGR of 2%. ADC costs ranged from $20-$85 with a median price of $180, which annualized to $15,600.

A home health aide median cost was $18 per hour for an annual price of $41,184 or $3,432 per month. Both these categories shared a 2% AGR.

A live-in homemaker/companion cost $39,308 annually, ranged from $10-$28/hour (median $17) yielding a $3,276 monthly median cost. This category had a 1% AGR.

Comparison and Conclusion as to the MetLife and Genworth Reports
Comparing the two reports, we see that the 2014 Genworth data for private-room SNF had a high of $271 per day, while the MetLife 2012 data included a low of $160 and a high of $450/day for a SNF in the Atlanta area. The 2014 Genworth data observed a low of $116 and a high of $271for a SNF private room. Here we see the difference at work between the observations reported and the methodology of reporting the median, versus the average of the data. Clearly, the Genworth report

considered fewer facilities than did the earlier MetLife report. We may as easily conclude that clearly the MetLife report was skewed toward observations made in the more metropolitan/densely populated areas of Georgia. But, both reports reflect similar annual growth rates across the categories. And both reports clearly reflect the reality of the very high costs of LTC. So, we conclude that the reports by and large support each other overall in terms of average costs. The 2014 divestment penalty divisor used by Georgia Department of Community Health, which administers the state's Medicaid program, is $5,825. This is the same number reported by Genworth as the median annual cost of care for a private room in a Georgia SNF. Without question, regardless of the report relied upon, these numbers are not only staggering, and they are significant because very few people are prepared to address these realities. Let's look at some risk management data to see the impact of these numbers.

Carriers Leaving the LTCi Arena

A 2010 Prudential research report estimated an annual growth rate for health care costs at 4.7% to 6.6%. These statistics jibe with the 2014 Genworth data showing AGRs in median costs of around 4%.

Depending on the type of services required over the past two years, Prudential broadened the estimated annual growth rate range to 2% to size 14% per year. These types of projections cause Prudential to make the decision to leave the group long-term care insurance ("LTCi") market effective August 1, 2012. Many other carriers followed suit. So what does that move tell us? Well, it tells us that big-name carriers are shying away from exposure to LTCi risk at least in the group policy arena. This is because those types of projected annual growth rates compounding the already scary numbers for SNF coverage could cause $5,672.71 per month to grow to $7,466.86 per month in five short years (60 months)! Even using the Genworth median AGRs of 4%, the SNF 2014 costs of $7,300/month would become $8,998/month in five years! That's a lot of exposure. So, the companies chose to leave the group policy LTCi arena rather than participate because of the overall mass exposure. Better to play in the individual markets, where premium charged can better ensure the carrier's risk/return profile remains manageable.

Individual Participation in the LTCi Marketplace

Moreover, the general population

has not prepared itself for this type of exposure either. Remember those survey questions I discussed with you previously? I polled those same audiences repeatedly over a three-month time period concerning whether or not those people currently had LTCi. Only 11% answered in the affirmative. A full 89% of respondents did not have LTCi. Curiously, 100% of those polled currently had auto accident insurance. Similarly, 93% had fire insurance in place. And yet the risk factor of one being involved in a major automobile accident is only 1 in 340. The risk from a total loss from fire is 1 in 1200. Yet, the risk of the person age 65 years of age or older needing LTCi, is 7 out of 10. These numbers were reported by the US Department of Health and Human Services, National Clearinghouse for Long-Term Care Information, www.long-term-care.gov, September 2008. Interestingly enough, and of special note to women, 70% of residents in SNFs are female, as reported by the AARP Pub. Policy Inst., "Fact Sheet: Women & Long-Term Care" April 2007. That same study reported that 70% of women were likely to be the primary caregiver for their parents in the parents' home or their own home. And of those women caregivers, 44%, almost half, reported high levels of physical strain or emotional stress as result of fulfilling the role of primary caregiver.

Now, reflect on the story that I told you in chapter 1 about what happened in my own family, what happened to my mother, and what happened to my sister when first my father fell victim to the stroke, and then when my mother fell victim to the stress caused as a result of my father having fallen victim to the stroke. Recall so what I pointed out was a major reason for the situation becoming as dire as it did - the failure to properly plan. Remember, I termed my dad's plan a "bet to die" strategy. It would be very astute of you at this point to recognize that, my father's plan was not working for him. So, then what might work for him would perhaps be the exact opposite of the strategy he was employing. If this is what occurred to you, then I applaud you for keeping pace with me. I am proposing a "bet to live" strategy. But Wally you may ask, you presented some very daunting facts about long-term care. You set forth a very dire and compelling, and even depressing case that appears to have no solution for most of us in the middle class. Let's start analyzing the planning process and look for possible solutions, because I did not bring you this far up the creek to leave you here without a paddle.

PART II
The Planning Process
&
The Search for Solutions

7

What Is Long-Term Care Planning?

We plan for all types of things: vacations, dinner with friends, birthday parties. I trust that at this point I haven't scared you with the harsh realities our generation faces. Rather, I hope that I have presented you with a case that establishes the need to plan for our future care. Allen Lakin, author and time management expert, defined the concept of planning by saying this,

"Planning is bringing the future and the present so you can do something about the future now." I don't think I've ever heard it more succinctly and aptly put. Applying that concept to our current situation at hand, we address the question, how will you pay for long-term care? In driving down to the bottom line, let's look at how our society at large is currently paying for long-term care.

Our society at large pays for LTC generally by using one of the following methods. The first 100 days are usually paid by Medicare. The first 20 days are 100% covered by Medicare, the next 80 are shared by you and Medicare, rather like a co-pay. Next, personal assets are liquidated in cash proceeds used to pay the bills; LTCi benefits kick in and start paying the bills after an elimination period is exhausted. Finally, children or other family members start liquidating their assets to pay for SNF bills for the institutionalized person. Usually, when no proper planning has been put in place, the bank of last resort is the United States federal government through the form of Medicaid is used to pay the bills and generally after all other avenues abruptly and exhausted. I say usually this is the plan of last resort because the qualification requirements for Medicaid benefits require a 60 month look-back at asset transfers, and the institutionalized person may have no more resources than $2,000 in their name. What a waste! With only proper planning, assets could be saved, dignity preserved, and family legacy restored. So, proper planning means planning to avoid certain calamities.

What we want to avoid is running out of money prematurely. We want to avoid leaving the home unprotected. We want to avoid risking the health and family or spousal caregivers. As I've stated repeatedly already family caregivers, especially spousal caregivers, are at far greater risk for serious health problems or death. There were approximately 10.9 million unpaid caregivers (family members and friends) providing care to persons with Alzheimer's or dementia in 2009. According to the Alzheimer's Association, those persons are at high risk of developing health problems, or worsening existing health issues. For example, family and other unpaid caregivers of people with Alzheimer's or another dementia are more likely than non-caregivers to have high levels of stress hormones, reduced immune function, slow wound healing, the hypertension, and coronary heart disease. Spouses who are caregivers for the other spouse with Alzheimer's or other dementia are at a greater risk for emergency room visits due to their health. A study mentioned in the 2010 Alzheimer's Association report on the caregivers of spouses who are hospitalized for dementia are more likely than caregivers of spouses who were hospitalized for other diseases, to die in the following year. Clearly then, proper planning must include making provisions for compensation of nonfamily caregivers in order to preserve the health of family members.

LTC planning is in many aspects

exactly the opposite of more traditional financial planning and wealth accumulation plan. Towards that end, let's look at the broadest part of the pyramid of LTC funding mechanisms first: Medicaid. Now there's a lot of street wisdom, urban legend and other "common knowledge" about Medicaid. Much of this misinformation about Medicaid stems from the complexities of the law itself, first passed in 1965 by Congress. The law has been seen is so convoluted that it was described like this by one United States Supreme Court opinion, "[Medicaid is] an aggravated assault on the English language, resistant to attempts to understand it." *Schweiker vs. Gray Panthers*, 453 US 34, 43 (1981). Part of this complication is due to the fact that Medicaid is a combination of both federal and state laws. The federal government funds the Medicaid program that is administered by each state. And each state has its own regulations for administration with in its own borders and jurisdiction. Thus, each states' requirements and rules and regulations will vary from those of other states. So now with that caveat, let's talk about Medicaid eligibility *in Georgia.*

8

Medicaid Planning at the State Level—Focus: Georgia

The truth about Medicaid eligibility is that you need to start planning at least more than 60 months ahead of the anticipated need for LTC benefits. Often, emergencies happen. When crises occur, my office can always help clients retain approximately half of their existing assets, *if we are engaged immediately*.

Unfortunately, the remainder of the assets will be required to be exhausted in order to comply with Medicaid eligibility rules. Setting aside the crisis case momentarily, let's just focus on the non-crisis planning situation.

First, a little terminology is in order. One term you need to be familiar with, is that used for the person placed in the LTC facility. We will call that person the *institutionalized person* or "IP." If that person is married, we will refer to that person as the *institutionalized spouse* or "IS." Secondly, for a married couple, we will term the spouse that is not in the LTC facility the *community spouse* or "CS." A common goal behind the federal Medicaid scheme is to prevent the CS from being impoverished. Lastly for now, the term "estate recovery" refers to that process whereby the state of Georgia attempts to recoup for the taxpayer, from the IS estate, after the death of both the IS and the CS, those dollars expended for the benefit of the IS. Currently, Georgia's policy is to pursue recovery where the estate is greater than or equal to $25,000 in resources, the recipients are older than 55 years of age, and received home and community-based services. The state will pursue all real property, including the home place. Note that recovery may be delayed in certain specific instances. Now with these understandings, let's look at what the IS gets to keep in Georgia in the non-crisis Medicaid planning context.

The law allows the IS to keep income up to $2,163 per month. The IS may keep up to $525,000 maximum equity in a personal residence. The IS may keep one car of any given value. The IS may keep all of his/her personal belongings (personal effects). The IS may keep prepaid funeral expenses contracts or insurance policies containing up to a $1,500 cash surrender value or the face value is $1,500 or less. A maximum of $10,000 face value of an insurance policy qualifies for the burial exclusion allowance. A term insurance policies face value is always counted first towards the burial exclusion. Only the face value may be applied towards the burial exclusion allowance, otherwise those amounts began counting as a resource. Life insurance policies with face amounts of greater than $10,000 must have the cash surrender value counted towards the resource limit. Ultimately, such policies may be subject to estate recovery absent proper planning. Transfers of the policy to another will incur a penalty based on the face value. Cashing-in will incur a penalty on the actual dollar amount. The IS may keep a small life insurance policy up to $1,500 face value. The big one: IS may keep up to $2,000 in assets/resources titled in the IS' name. The biggest one: all assets transferred out of your name within 5 years of the date the Medicaid application is submitted are not counted against the IS as a resource.

So, Medicaid has a 60-month look-back period during which all asset transfers, including gifts, are analyzed for whether or not such were exchanges for value, or stated another way, were fair market value exchanges. If not, a penalty period is imposed for transfer violation. Now, what that means is, the IS will have to pay his or her own expenses for a certain period of time that relates to the dollar amount of the "gift" or transfer that was in violation of the regulations, before the Medicaid benefits will kick in.

These rules were imposed by the Deficit Reduction Act of 2005 (DRA '05). The DRA also imposed restrictions on the use of annuities. Now, only certain very special types of annuities may be used in the Medicaid process and avoid being counted as a resource or otherwise penalized. These specialized types of annuities are called "Medicaid compliant annuities." Any type of annuities sold to a person age 70 years old or older must be analyzed in terms of proper Medicaid planning, or else the vendor who sold such annuity runs the risk of committing professional error. Otherwise, the purchaser runs the risk of having to liquidate early said annuity and then re-purchasing a Medicaid compliant annuity. Obviously, this will involve substantial cash penalties in terms of the early cashing out of the previous "standard" annuity, and may include tax liabilities as well. This is why any financial planner who advises the purchase of anything less than a Medicaid compliant annuity to any person age 70 years or older without ensuring that that person's Medicaid planning will support such a purchase, should immediately contact his or her E&O insurer if the purchaser or their family comes to my law office for planning. I will advise them of a potential claim and cause of action and then be more than willing to pursue same to conclusion on behalf of the elder and family.

9

Paying for LTC—The LTC Timeline and Insurance

Now let's view long-term care planning as though we could progress smoothly along a timeline. The ideal progression would be from In-Home/In-Place Aging into Assisted Living and then into Skilled Nursing long-term care. Life usually isn't so cooperative. Still, "I want to go to a nursing home!" is not something we can expect anyone to say, ever! Most people want to age in place.

This is not surprising, and fits in well with the values of independence so central to the core of the American culture. So, it's important that we apply for long-term care benefits only when we have to, or when it becomes the most advantageous to us. Often, this is at the same time. The timing of the application is of paramount importance when one applies for Medicaid benefits. But, we are in the business of creating options, not deadlines. Let's look at what options are currently available so at least we have an idea of what's on the horizon, should we be so fortunate to encounter it. It goes without saying that if a person has resources, they will self-fund these necessities, at least until the resources have been exhausted. But what if we could qualify for benefits without exhausting all resources? The good news is that the government has enacted laws that allow us to do so, legally. Let's get some perspective on some of these options.

First let's take a look at in-home aging. Georgia has a program called, "Money Follows the Person." To qualify for this program and still receive benefits while aging in-home in place, a person must first be Medicaid eligible and must meet a variety of other stated criteria. MFP provides funding benefits for improvements to both the house and an automobile. These benefits also pay for any in-home services required. Obviously, if these are being state-funded, then the person has qualified for assistance and is not entirely self-funding these necessities. What happens if in-home aging is no longer an option? At this juncture, the next step along the timeline is Assisted Living Facilities ("ALFs") and Skilled Nursing Facilities ("SNF"). Costs are naturally going to increase. So, let's get some perspective on how we can best plan for those consequences.

Self-Funding LTC Expenses

We'll get into the cost of Medicaid qualification and the process in terms of planning for Medicaid qualifications more in depth later in this chapter. But, what if a person wants to self-fund their long-term care? While there are a couple of options. One option, the most obvious, is to have a significant amount of either liquid assets or easily convertible assets that can be exhausted over time to satisfy the costs of long-term care. Second, and perhaps the wiser of the options available, is to purchase long-term care insurance.

An initial problem of purchasing

long-term care insurance is determining the best age to buy that long-term care insurance ("LTCi"). We can do a quick comparison of the cost of waiting by analogizing with the same criteria we us to purchase technology. As we've seen over the past several years, the cost of electronics today made them quite expensive when a gadget first comes out, and are likely to drop in price dramatically, sometimes after they've been out for a year or 2. In comparison, applying this methodology to the purchase of LTCi is often quite disadvantageous and quite costly. In simplest terms, you have to build the Ark before it starts raining. If you are in need of LTCi, the companies that provide that product will consider you uninsurable and prohibit you from purchasing a policy. So, you have to buy the insurance while still healthy. If your health deteriorates, insurance companies charge a premium, sometimes 13% to 70.5% more for the same level of coverage. If long-term care costs continue rising at the same inflation rate, you may need to buy 5% or more coverage each year you delay your purchase. As you grow older, insurance companies charge more for the same level of coverage. Some states have minimum purchase requirements for the partnership programs (which are long-term care insurance policies to protect assets away from Medicaid). Some states, including California and Connecticut, increase their minimum purchase requirements by 5% each year, thus, increasing the price by 5%. Insurance companies regularly raise rates for new applicants, often times 10 to 30%. So, as always with insurance, the younger you are the lower your premiums. LTCi companies price policies to reflect the risk. So the longer an insurer collects and invests your premiums, the lower the insurance company's risk, the lower your annual premiums, and the lower your cumulative premiums paid to age 85. The companies publish cost of waiting tables to show prices of various ages.

Now the best data available (these data was taken from Genworth statistics published for 2014) show the cost of waiting since 2011 has risen over the past three years. Appendix Table 1 Cost of Waiting to Buy LTCi shows the annual premium, comparing the premiums of page to age 85, and the cost of waiting one, 5, or 10 years.

The table reflects benefits of $200 per day of care for 5 years, with a 5% compound inflation protection, and a 90 day elimination period (note that the elimination period is effectively your "co-pay"). This is for a 50-year-old husband and wife, per person. Delaying the purchase from age 50 to 55, increases the annual premium by $1,226 and the cumulative premiums paid to age 85 by $22,565. The lesson to be learned from this table is that long-term care insurance (LTCi) should be purchased between the ages of 50 and 60 years and daily benefits need to be locked in at a minimum of $200 today per day of benefit, ranging to $326. Obviously, the cost of waiting just three years from 2011 to 2014 increased premiums by well over half. Still, the 10 year LTCi companies' costs of waiting tables do not emphasize one critical point. Although the cost of waiting tables portray the price of policies and the cost of waiting, they do not emphasize enough the higher rates companies charge new applicants of the same age and health when they introduced the pricing. For example, the cost of waiting 2011 table that was published at the end of 2011, indicates a 50-year-old would have paid $64,210 of cumulative premiums if paid to age 85. Less than 2.5 years later, the cost of waiting until 2014 table indicates a 50-year-old paid $99,541 of total premiums. That's a 55% increase, or $35,331 more in paid premiums for the same benefit!

The obvious solution then is to purchase your LTCi now, to ensure yourself that you're paying the lowest price. Any of the 6 items listed above can lead to your paying significantly more for your policy. There's only one item that is certain on the list of 6 items: in one year's time, you will be one year older. Still, you need to understand all 6 items when purchasing LTCi. Accordingly, purchase your LTCi policy when you're young and healthy, thereby assuring that you will pay the lowest price possible. Feel free to contact my financial advisory service for more information and get a free quote on

LTCi coverage for you and/or your spouse or other family member by contacting Asset Guidance Group, LLC, at 404-348-4120. You may also email me at nicholsw@ceteranetworks.com. (Suitability is paramount for investments of any type. All investments are not suitable for every person or group. Attorney-client privilege does not attach to any insurance or investment related disclosures as such information must be disclosed to non-attorney third parties.)

10

Paying for LTC—Asset Protection & Medicaid Planning

Let's now move into some estate planning concepts for the other end of the spectrum: Medicaid planning, Medicaid asset protection planning and Veteran's Administration ("VA") Aid & Attendance Planning. What we look for here is to establish the proper criteria to protect a person's estate from the risk exposure of LTC. To do so, we engage in liability limiting asset transfers after doing some legal entity creation. One aspect of this type of estate planning is the use of a Medicaid asset protection trust, or what I like to term as a "Medicaid compliant, liability limiting trust." Here, we bridge the gap through the 60 month "look back" period imposed pursuant to Medicaid law by legal entity creation and then investing available assets to preserve resources for later use or legacy planning. As discussed in the previous section, we may also explore the options of using investment/funding of insurance needs, one of which is LTCi, the other is by life insurance hybrid.

This is all part of a process we employ to develop an aging in place plan. We establish that plan, and define the funding required to put that plan into effect. Of course, as we progress along the implementation timeline, we take steps at our firm to ensure that all appropriate legal mechanisms are kept evergreen and provide the client with an option to ensure that this maintenance is updated every 2 to 3 years and that the documents are electronically available, if the client so desires.

First, let me take you on a brief detour to give you the fundamentals of a basic estate plan. Then, we'll return to the main thoroughfare and review the use of these more advanced estate planning techniques to ensure preservation of assets for family legacy, while maintaining eligibility for public or VA assistance benefits. Always keep in mind that the primary purpose of this type of planning is to give you options, when otherwise you may have none. Options are quite comforting during periods of high stress—just imagine an escape hatch when the monsters have you backed into a corner, and otherwise there would be no way out but one!

11

Basic Planning for Everyone

Before delving into the more advanced topics, it behooves me to give you an understanding of the basic essentials of the well-planned estate. An extremely important part of the basic estate planning process is simply to look at how to avoid probate in terms of death okay so we do that initially through the use of revocable living trust ("RLT”). By employing a RLT, we add value by eliminating the delay of probate, which even under a comparatively simplified process such as Georgia's current scheme, which requires at a minimum: filing the probate, including the original last will and testament in local public record, noticing the filing to potential heirs, beneficiaries and creditors, and probable publication of the probate in a local newspaper for several consecutive weeks. The family still must endure the loss of privacy associated with making the deceased's last will and testament, normally a private document, a part of public record, as well as paying attorney fees for the probate.

In comparison, the RLT format avoids probate for the most important parts of the estate, if not the entire estate. Conventionally, the RLT has been used to mitigate estate taxes upon the death of the first spouse. This planning remains in effect for large estates. But, as of the time of this writing, the federal estate tax exemption is $5.34 million per spouse ($10.68 million per married couple). So, for most middle-class families, the greatest benefit of the RLT is asset protection and privacy preservation. In the age of the internet, where predators can review local county legal organs (publications where legal notices are published) and then follow up with internet searches, the premium on the latter benefit cannot be overstated.

The traditional RLT plan provides for the trust-maker (the "Grantor") to remain in control of his/her/their assets until the death of the first spouse. Then, assets are split and at least one additional trust springs into existence to handle the transfer or preservation of the deceased's share of assets to the children or other important persons to the deceased, while the surviving spouse remains in control of the remainder of assets in his/her own RLT. This children's trust, or family trust, or whatever name by which it is known, should be an irrevocable trust with appropriate provisions to provide asset protection to its beneficiaries.

Upon the death of the second or surviving spouse, the assets that were held in that person's RLT are passed to his/her beneficiaries in trust, with the same or similar provisions as with the first-to-die in order to properly protect the beneficiaries from third parties, creditors and so forth. The potential tax and other implications of these downstream trusts are beyond the scope of this brief introduction and indeed could warrant entire chapters on them alone. For now, suffice it to say that dynastic provisions are possible and other protective provisions are amazing legacies to pass on to successive generations and beneficiaries. But a fundamental value here lies in the avoidance of probate and the potential for litigation that consumes chunks of the assets to be passed on. That value alone could save a family $750-$2,500 or more in attorney fees and costs, not to mention the time delays in transferring assets.

In summation, the RLT contains the fundamentals of estate planning, and in any sport, championships are won by those successfully implementing the fundamentals.

Ancillary Documents

Beyond the basics, our firm creates "supercharged" powers of attorney, which include HIPAA authorizations, advance healthcare directives, and financial powers of attorney.
Advance healthcare directives include options required by statute, as well as, for example, whether or not a person wants to be an organ donor, whether or not a person desires an autopsy to determine the cause of death, or states that in no event should there be an autopsy to determine the cause of death. A proper Directive contains provisions for “Do Not Resuscitate”

("DNR)"/"Do Not Intubate" ("DNI") orders.

The Last Will & Testament

I view the traditional "Last Will & Testament" as an ancillary document. This is because it is not the center-piece of the estate plan. In all events, the estate plan should include a last will and testament simply to cover any remaining or what I term "residue" assets and debts. Out of necessity, there will be assets that are remaining outside of a trust because of timing issues, transfer delays, funding delays, and the like. The Will is to sweep these assets, which ideally are of minimal importance, into the hands of the appropriate beneficiaries. Thus, the Will is merely the broom that sweeps the crumbs that are left after the dinner party has concluded. To accomplish this task, a probate filing is required. But, if we've done our job appropriately, this probate will be a summary proceeding and quite expeditious.

12

Advanced Planning Techniques

A Medicaid Compliant Liability Limiting Trust is a specially designed irrevocable trust that transfers a defined amount of assets from the trust-maker ("Grantor") to third parties, usually family members such as children, for the purposes of qualifying for Medicaid benefits to pay long-term care costs. Similarly, a VA Liability Limiting Trust is a specially designed irrevocable trust that transfers a defined amount of assets from the Grantor to third parties, usually family members such as children, for the purposes of qualifying for VA Aid & Attendance ("A&A") benefits to pay for long-term care assistance. VA A&A benefits are available to war-time veterans who require assistance with more than two activities of daily living ("ADLs"). The income tax on income derived by such trusts is paid for by the Grantor at the lower individual tax rates. These trusts' primary purpose is to accomplish the spend-down required by Medicaid law and by VA regulations. But, instead of the spend-down being exhausted on third-party healthcare providers, the spend-down is transferred to the Grantor's intended beneficiaries. The trusts are irrevocable because Medicaid law requires the trusts to be irrevocable. Stated another way, a revocable trust will not comply with Medicaid law nor VA regulations. For those reasons, provisions must carefully be planned and calculated to reach the precise optimum amount of assets and income that both go into the trust, irrevocably, and that are retained by the Grantor or the marital community spouse (the "Community Spouse, or CS").

In crisis situations, we distinguish between the CS and the

institutionalized spouse ("IS"), because one of the primary drivers behind the Medicaid law is the public policy that the CS should not be forced into impoverishment simply due to paying for the care required by the IS. Certain other types of special irrevocable trusts may be required in order to ensure that the IS or Medicaid applicant meets all Medicaid qualification rules, both in terms of total resources available, and ongoing income level limits.

Rather than getting you bogged down into technical details, an example is a great way of demonstrating these concepts in action.

A Hypothetical Illustration

Let's look at one example here of Mary's story as an illustration of how this process works:

Mary was a 78-year-old woman who recently lost her husband after a long battle with cancer. Her family wanted to make sure that she would be taken care of in case her health should fail. Mary’s two children live in different states. So, they are unable to closely monitor Mary's well-being personally. They worry about her living alone. Mary owns a home and approximately $225,000 in checking, savings, and CDs.

Mary had a long-term care policy that she had been paying for the last 20 years. The LTCi will pay a daily benefit of $75.

Here's Mary's aging in place plan. First, we decided that she should definitely keep the LTCi policy. Next, we place a portion of Mary's liquid assets, $175,000, and her home into an irrevocable family trust that her children would oversee and get funds from if needed. Next, it was most optimum for Mary to keep $50,000 in a revocable trust that Mary would use for home repairs, vacations, or anything else that she wanted. Now, take note that we have used both kinds of trusts I explained to you above: Mary created an irrevocable trust for the family that the children could oversee and get funds from if needed, and Mary also created a revocable trust to hold assets at her ready disposal to do with as she pleased, yet remained free from probate worries.

Remember what I just said in the preceding sections above? The basic fundamentals of estate planning are going to always set forth at least a revocable living trust, sometimes coupled with an irrevocable living trust, as set forth in this example. The reason for this is that we want to avoid probate hassles at all costs.

Why you may ask, Georgia has a very lenient and efficient and easy to manage probate system? While I may agree with you that at least in theory the statute provides for expedited probate in Georgia, the most important factor that we have in a modern society is that of privacy. Especially with the advent of technology, we must put a premium on the price of our privacy. With the Internet and in the Internet age, anyone can find out anything about anyone or everyone. The advancement of medical science and the technologies that it has provided us not only have enabled us to stay alive longer through the use of technology in medical science, but this is a two-edged sword. For, the longevity technology has provided us is also the downside cost. There is never a free lunch. First, we can't outlive our money and that is a real danger. Second, we don't want our children to be burdened with paying for our expenses, as they have a tough enough economy as it is. Third, is that our privacy is susceptible of being exploited by anyone searching public records. Now, how you say that they will do that Wally? Well, believe it or not, there are people that make a living out of perusing each county's probate records and then soliciting those survivors and those family members named in the death or obituary columns and probate records. They can do this because you have to file a last will in the probate court which then becomes public record—you are required to file the Will, it is not a choice. In that Will a person's most private intimate details about their assets and family members is clearly set forth. So if we use a revocable trust we offset the need for ever probating that Will and making that type of information or any type of detailed information about anyone's assets available to the public. That's the kind of protection our clients deserve and that's the protection our firm provides through the use of different types of legal entities, primarily trusts. Because a trust is merely a contract between you and yourself about what is to happen with your property, it is not required to be probated. Therefore, the entirety of your estate can be distributed as you saw fit when you created the trust, in the same way that you created the trust: on our conference room table. Thus, no one need ever know the intimate details of how you distribute your estate. Behold the elegance of estate planning with the use of trusts!

Now back to Mary story, we also created supercharged powers of attorney for health and financial decisions. So the result is that if Mary's health should fail, she will have the long-term care policy, her own funds and her children will have access to the family trust funds. After 5 years at most, all of the assets in the family trust, $175,000, would be protected and would not be counted for Medicaid purposes should Mary need residential long-term care. Note: this family trust is an irrevocable trust it has to comply with the Medicaid laws similar to the special types of annuities I described earlier in this chapter - these types of entities have to be Medicaid-compliant.

If Mary becomes unable to make decisions for herself, the financial and healthcare agents that she named in the powers of attorney will step in to make decisions on Mary's behalf in accordance with the terms that Mary set forth.

Now if Mary had done nothing, her home and all of the liquid assets ($225,000), would have been consumed by long-term care costs. If Mary did not have a proper financial power of attorney, thousands of dollars could have been spent on setting up a guardianship/conservatorship for her, and the court would have decided who makes decisions for her. That cost alone is going to average somewhere between $1,500 and $2,500 or more, depending upon the size of any individual estate. Here, given Mary's assets, let's assume that the probate costs and attorney's fees for setting up a guardianship on doing the paperwork and making the hearing and doing the appropriate follow-up work would average somewhere between $1,500-$2,500. Thus, merely setting up the financial powers of attorney alone and the health care directive saved the estate that money. Further, there would be no funds that her children could use to make sure Mary is getting the best care possible that nothing would pass to them upon her death. Why you ask? Well, because the assets would have been exhausted paying for Mary's health care.

Again, our goals here are to age with dignity, to access the best care possible, to take control over who will manage finances if you're unable to, and specify under what conditions circumstances that the persons you empower to do so, will in fact be able to do so. The ultimate goal is to leave a legacy that you choose, not what the state or your health care providers choose for you.

13

Crisis Planning

If you recall the initial story of my parents' situation, by the time that we were able to finally accomplish the plan for my dad, my mother had already exhausted a huge portion of his liquid estate (read, "cash") paying for his care. Accordingly, since we could not satisfy the requirement of the transfers of assets being 60 months in the past, we had to do crisis planning in my father's situation. Frequently, we find we can save roughly half of a person's estate and still qualify for Medicaid even when they have failed to properly plan, as was the case with my parents. It's definitely better to save about half the estate, than to save none of the estate. I mean, my father worked hard all his life to save what little he had. We could think of no harsher outcome than to have to exhaust all of those assets to pay for his healthcare and assisted living expenses. Yet, this is what all my mother's trusted friends and advisors told her was the only course of action—unfortunately they could see no other outcome but for her to completely zero out all the accounts by paying the nursing home, pharmacy and doctors. Well, not if I could help it! But first, I had to persuade my parents to listen to and trust me.

Sometimes the hardest thing for parents of that generation is to listen to their own children or take advice or help. See, e.g., http://www.forbes.com/sites/carolynrosenblatt/2014/09/09/no-easy-task-getting-aging-parents-to-accept-help/. My father was willing, while my mother was reluctant. Eventually, she came around to the reality that doing something was far better than doing nothing. She was willing to at least try, albeit fearfully willing. Sad, but that's how it goes with some people in some families.

At this point, however, it behooves me to reiterate that these planning techniques we use are time-proven and court-tested. It's not like I was experimenting—I knew what needed to be done and I've practiced law for well over 20 years. But, persuading those involved—here my mother—proved more difficult and time consuming than in most other cases, certainly more burdensome than it needed to be. Sometimes, people are fearful of change. Sometimes, people are unaccustomed to decision-making or the decision-making process. Often, people have fragile egos and are unfamiliar with many of the terms, legal, financial, medical, and this dynamic only adds to the problem. These are yet others in a long list of reasons why planning for long-term care should be undertaken in a controlled environment, in the best of times.

With crisis planning, you are dealing with a pressured situation and a dynamic environment in the worst of times, and with little time on your side. These realities are all working against one's ability and decrease greatly the probabilities of making "the" optimal decision, much less "an" optimal decision. When faced with this situation, again which is the result of the failure to make these planning decisions ahead of time, we do the best we can do with the facts that we have, given that the law is established and in place. The responsible thing to do is set aside all these ego and personality issues early on in the aging process, and deal with the realities one faces in a responsible, mature fashion—one commensurate with one's age and the gravity of the consequences. Alas, that's not what we have to work with as professionals dealing with the crisis situation. So, what did we do? Well, we employed our experience, training and professional associates to develop the best plan we could craft under the circumstances.

First, we had to get a comprehensive listing of all assets and fair market value of each. This "marshaling of the assets" is a time-intensive undertaking and without good organization, can be quite a frustrating experience when time is not a factor, so it becomes a multiplier on the frustration meter when time is of the essence!

Before we could begin moving assets, we had to have a "bucket" to hold them. So next, we created a Medicaid compliant liability limiting trust into which my mother could transfer assets. Once we had the "bucket" in place to hold the assets, next, we had to liquidate the annuities that some misguided (and undoubtedly self-interested) financial advisor had sold him when my father was around age 75. These existing annuities were not Medicaid compliant. So, we had to convert these resources and cash streams into one cash stream that was Medicaid compliant. In this fashion, my mother's assets would be protected as she continues to age alongside my father. More importantly in the short term, this step was necessary so that these assets would not be counted as resources against my dad's Medicaid qualification.

Of course, there were severe tax consequences associated with this liquidation and transfer, but it was a necessary decision. These transfers were much akin to swallowing a poison pill. Again, this is the harsh reality of failing to responsibly plan ahead of time. There are consequences to irresponsible behavior and I maintain that failing to plan ahead of time is irresponsible behavior.

In this case, the financial analysis showed it was necessary to eat a one-time $5,000-$7,500 potential tax liability, rather than to continue to pay the monthly costs of care for my dad's long-term care needs. Those costs, were averaging around $6,100 per month. Although the liquidation created a $7,500 tax liability, that meant only of a loss of one to one and a half months' worth of paying for my father's long-term care expenses. The result: my dad ultimately qualified for Medicaid even though we made those transfers within 60 months of submitting his Medicaid application. No longer was my mother required to write those huge checks to the nursing home at the first of each month. Instead, she now had a cash stream that grew in her own banking accounts that she could count on each month until the new annuity paid out: better to bank $5,000+ per month than pay it out!

We protected the house for my mother to continue to reside in, as well as the assets that she was able to retain as the community spouse (CS). Of course, we also had to analyze all the asset transfers that had occurred during the 60 months (5 years) immediately preceding the time my father had to check into the nursing home. We had to get a precise picture of the entire financial situation so that we could get a calculation to enable us to precisely, surgically, and professionally, quantify the exact amount required to make the plan work in accord with the law. Then we could divide and transfer the assets—ideally all at once. You really only get one shot at this, so it has to be right! Finally came the Medicaid application.

This whole process took the better part of the year, but the results were phenomenal in terms of my mother's ensuing happiness, her peace of mind, her well-being, and that of my brother, my sister, and me. My dad was so pleased that we worked it all out, and he continues to this day to receive long-term care which costs on the average $5,000-$6,000 per month, including medications, plus room and board and other assistance that he requires for his ADLs. The difference is that my mother no longer is exhausting their assets with the monthly expenditures that were going to the SNF. Instead, she has been able to rebuild her own checking and savings accounts as time goes by. All in all, since that first year passed, my parents' estate saved almost $72,000 for that one $7,500 tax liability. Of course, we don't take that penalty lightly, and no one wants to take a poison pill. But, these are the prices one pays for failing to properly plan ahead, and thus allowing the crisis situation to arise in the first place.

One has to build the ark before it starts raining; an ounce of prevention is worth a pound of cure. Here, we had no choice but to make lemonade out of our lemons. We had to make the best out of a bad situation. I urge that we did fairly well in the final analysis: Would you pay $7,500 to get an immediate cash stream of that would be the equivalent of $73,200 in 12 months? You bet you would! Anyone would be foolish not to take that deal. And that deal gets sweeter with each passing month that my mom doesn't have to pay another $5,000+ check to the nursing home for my dad's care.

Now, my mom can envision how she can maintain her own financial independence as she and my father continue to age. My dad was ecstatic that he was no longer a burden to my mother in terms of finances, because he could not do what he had done his entire life (and they had been married most of their lives - they recently celebrated their 70th wedding anniversary!) as the financial provider. Instead, we saved the money that he had indeed earned during his income producing years and prevented it from being exhausted solely to pay doctors and long-term care facilities. We got him the benefits to which he was entitled as an American taxpayer all those years of his working life: Medicaid. That's good stewardship!

Now, we are diligently monitoring and cultivating those assets he worked so hard for his entire life. We want to ensure that the most important thing to my father, his legacy, is preserved and passed on to subsequent generations, just as he wished and instructed me it should be. That's good stewardship! The most important thing a person can do is to plant trees the shade of he/she knows they themselves will never sit, but that subsequent generations will! That's good stewardship in the form of sharing. Anything less, is unabashed narcissism—selfishness has never been a moral virtue in any culture.

Speaking of morals, this planning is also moral, legal, and ethical. Congress has maintained and the courts have upheld for the better part of 50 years that the CS is not to be impoverished by the long-term care costs of the IS. The unmistakable congressional intent was to provide for the CS, and save the estate for the IS' legacy, thereby allowing dignity at the end stage of life by preserving a legacy to be passed on to the IS' descendants.

So, in the final analysis, my father's assets were preserved to the extent the law allowed, my mother's financial security cemented into place as best we could, and everyone's peace of mind restored. Implementation of the plan greatly reduced my mother's stress, as well as that of my father just worrying about my mother and how she was going to make it. Because there was nothing he could do about his care expenses. In that aspect, their story ended much like the movies that they enjoyed in their young adult years: the cowboy riding off into the sunset with the girl and both living happily ever after. Because, if my mother's health should fail, like Mary, she has her own funds set aside in her account that she can do with as she chooses. We also have the funds preserved in the family trust. All those family trust assets will be protected and preserved as a legacy from her and my dad. None of those funds will be counted against her Medicaid qualification should she wind up needing residential long-term care in a SNF. When she's unable to make decisions for herself, both my sister and I are in place on her financial and healthcare powers of attorney, thereby avoiding the probate process, probate expenses, and the compromise of privacy associated with the probate process. That outcome is the desired result from proper planning.

So, if you haven't already learned it by now from this story, know this: advance planning yields better, less stressful results than crisis planning. Planning ahead of time is the mature thing to do; it's the responsible thing to do. Thus, it's the right thing to do!

14

VA Aid & Attendance Planning

We covered a lot of ground here, but this work would be incomplete if we omitted a discussion of the veteran administration aid and attendance benefit. The VA Aid and Attendance benefit is an increased monthly pension amount that can be added to a veteran's monthly pension if they meet certain conditions. The A&A benefit is not technically a pension, it is a non-service-connected disability assistance benefit. The A&A pension benefit is one of the most underutilized benefits that the VA offers to wartime veterans and their widows. While the A&A benefit is a special pension benefit available to help veterans who served during a war time or their widows pay for their Medical Care, medical supplies, and medicines from the VA, there are asset and income limits that must be met in order to qualify for these benefits. As such, careful planning needs to be employed in order to maximize or optimize the veteran's or widow(er)'s overall resource and income picture without exhausting the vast majority of their financial wherewithal.

To qualify, the war veteran must have served 90 consecutive days on active military duty one day of which was during a war period. Importantly, there is no requirement that any service be performed at a combat zone. Veteran must have received a better than dishonorable discharge in order to qualify. A widow or widower must not have divorced the veteran or remarried after the veteran's death. The veteran or widow(er) ("Claimant") must be certified by a doctor as needing assistance with 2 or more ADLs. Specific examples of ADLs are:

- Claimant requires the aid of another person in order to perform personal functions required in everyday living, such as bathing, feeding, dressing, attending to the wants of nature, adjusting prosthetic devices, or protecting themselves from the hazards of their daily environment;

- Claimant is bedridden, and that claimant's disability or disabilities requires that they remain in bed apart from any prescribed course of convalescence or treatment;

- Claimant is a patient in a nursing home due to mental or physical incapacity;

- Claimant's eyesight is limited to a corrected 5/200 visual acuity or less in both eyes, or concentric contraction of the visual field to 5° or less;

- Claimant is housebound. If Claimant is substantially confined to his or her immediate premises because of permanent disability, Claimant is considered by the VA to be "housebound."

The household must have significantly less than a certain amount of allowable countable assets in order to qualify. Currently this nebulous amount, which is subject to the discretion of the VA, has been considered to be somewhere in a range significantly less than $80,000. Yet, there is no hard and fast rule or settled amount that can be fully relied upon without argument. This is why experienced, competent counsel is important to have to advocate on the Claimant's behalf. Lastly, the adjusted household income, which is the gross household income less all unreimbursed recurring medical expenses, must be less than the A&A benefit.

So, it is safe to say that the A&A benefits, adjusted household income, and allowable countable assets, all must fall within or below acceptable ranges or threshold amounts—amounts that are somewhat fluid and are set at the VA's discretion frequently case-by-case. With proper planning, the Claimant can qualify for A&A while preserving their household assets and still qualify for Medicaid if necessary. This will aid the family in paying for medical care and postpone the depletion of the Claimant's assets. The goal is to stretch the assets so the family can postpone the need to reply upon Medicaid to pay for healthcare.

The VA also has robust ancillary benefits available to claimants who have service or non-service connected disabilities. For example, there is a Home Improvements In Structural Alterations ("HISA") grant available that pays up to $2,000 for claimants to improve a home, in order to make it accessible. If the veteran's disability is service-connected, there are two grants available the Special Adapted Housing ("SAH") grant is in excess of $6,000 and the Specially Housing Adaption ("SHA") grant is really big--

$67,555! This is why it's important to have not only an advocate to assist the claimant in navigating VA bureaucracy, not just anyone can do it. The VA specifically requires accreditation for attorneys before that attorney is allowed to represent claimants before a VA administrative panel. Moreover, accredited attorneys must continue to maintain their competency by attending by annual continuing legal education to ensure they are current in the law, both substantively and procedurally, in so far as representing veterans and claimants before the VA.

The 2014 pension benefit figures for

wartime veterans are set out in Table 2 Max VA Benefit Parameters of the Appendix.

Periodically, issues arise stemming from the complex interaction of VA benefits and Medicaid qualification. So the astute reader might well ask whether a choice must be made between one benefit programs. Better still, one might ask whether qualification under one program might preclude qualification for the other. Since it's traditionally been more expedient for a veteran to first qualify for the improved pension and A&A benefit and then deal with Medicaid issues, the question is pointedly whether the income derived from the VA benefits would then be considered as countable income for Medicaid qualification purposes. Thanks to my affiliation with ElderCounsel®, CEO Valerie Peterson, and its elite group of member attorneys, one in particular being nationally renowned Medicaid litigator, Rene Reixach, we learn that in a June, 2014 case from New Jersey has shined a definitive light on this rather murky topic.

Galletta v. Velez (D.N.J. June 3, 2014), held that if payments of VA benefits resulting from "unusual medical expenses," then they should be disregarded for as income for Medicaid qualification purposes regardless of whether the VA categorized them as A&A or VA improved pension benefits. *Galletta* reasoned that federal law required consistency between the Medicaid program Supplemental Security Income program and the VA. Thus, where SSI excluded from countable income to qualify for that program's benefits, VA benefits received because of "unusual medical expenses," then the Medicaid agency could not include those benefits as countable income for Medicaid qualification purposes. The end result in that situation was that the claimant qualified for VA improved pension benefits, VA A&A benefits, and Medicaid benefits. So what constitutes "unusual medical expenses?" Well, that's the art of the deal – the essence of what I do. See how great it is to have competent counsel affiliated with national organizations so that he stays on the cutting edge of these legal issues!

Presently, unlike Medicaid, the VA does not have any rules that restrict the form of asset transfers in order to accomplish spend-down, or a look-back period. Having said that, a caveat is in order. Two pieces of legislation have been meandering their way through the United States Congress on these issues. I am writing this work in 2014, a midterm election year. So, while these bills may not go into law this year, they will undoubtedly be reviewed when the new Congress is seated in 2015. Senate Bill 748 was incorporated into Senate Bill 944 pursuant to recommendations made by the Senate Committee on Veterans Affairs earlier this year. These recommendations specifically will put in place both a look-back period and penalty provisions for asset transfers occurring within a certain timeframe when that Bill reaches the Senate floor. Another bill, Senate Bill 1982, also contains look-back and penalty provisions. So, in an era of fiscal restraint, deficit reduction focus, and budgetary concerns, it is highly probable that this legislation will be passed by the Senate and transferred to the House of Representatives before or shortly after the next presidential election in 2016. Thus, not only should any potential claimant feel a sense of urgency about starting the process, the planning is clearly more complex and going to be more difficult to push through the VA bureaucracy in order to successfully obtain the benefits to which the claimant is rightfully entitled. Competent legal counsel is therefore indispensable, and the time to take action is now before the laws change!

15

Conclusions

What do we see from all the items discussed at this point? What should be most apparent is that the best time to move forward with planning is now. We should take advantage of all the current high gift tax exemptions that the tax laws madke available (which are currently $10.4 million) and get all future appreciation of your taxable estate. Both estate tax and asset protection laws, as well as Medicaid laws and Medicare laws and VA Aid & Attendance regulations, as set forth in the United States code and elsewhere, may change in the future. Currently, the United States Senate Committee on Veteran's Affairs has been considering putting in place a three-year look-back provision for Aid & Attendance benefits as well as income limitations. Congress has had discussion in various committees concerning possible extension of the 5-year look-back period for Medicaid. It goes without saying that were all living in an age of budget cutbacks, budgetary constraints, and deficit reduction legislation at both the federal and state levels. Since 2008, there has been pressure on governments due to the lack of resources at the state and local levels. We've already seen that crisis planning is difficult, leads to unnecessary loss and expenses, and a less than optimum outcome. Crisis planning is the cure for stubbornness and selfishness, both unnecessary and undesirable traits for a well-lived and balanced life generally, but especially so in the end-stages of life when estate and financial planning are essential. Better to get one's house in order before the storm hits. In the words of one of the most famous baby-boomers, "The Times, They Are a Changin'!" So, the worst choice as always is procrastination.

APPENDIX

Table 1

Cost of Waiting 2011						Cost of Waiting 2014			Premium Increase 2014 v 2011
When Purchased	Age	Daily Benefit	Annual Premium		If Paid to Age 85	Cost of Waiting	Annual Premium	If Paid to Age 85	Cost of Waiting
Today	50	$200	$1,835	$64,210	$0	$2,844	$99,541	$0	55%
In 1 Year	51	$210	$1,941	$66,005	$1,795	$3,059	$104,018	$4,478	58%
In 5	55	$255	$2,485	$74,558	$10,348	$4,070	$122,106	$22,566	64%
In 10 Years	60	$326	$4,014	$100,345	$36,135	$5,455	$136,386	$36,846	36%

Table 2

Type of Benefit	**Maximum Annual Pension Rate (Income Limit)**	**Monthly Maximum Annual Pension Rate (Income Limit)**
Service Pension	$12,652 Medical expenses must exceed $632 to be deducted	$1,054 Medical expenses must exceed $52 to be deducted

Type of Benefit	**Maximum Annual Pension Rate (Income Limit)**	**Monthly Maximum Annual Pension Rate (Income Limit)**
One Dependent	$16,569 Medical expenses must exceed $828 to be deducted	$1,381 Medical expenses must exceed $69 to be deducted
Housebound	$15,462	$1,288
One Dependent	$19,380	$1,615

Type of Benefit	**Maximum Annual Pension Rate (Income Limit)**	**Monthly Maximum Annual Pension Rate (Income Limit)**
Aid & Attendance	$21,107	$1,758
One Dependent	$25,022	$2,085
Each add'l dependent child	$2,161	$180

Type of Benefit	**Maximum Annual Pension Rate (Income Limit)**	**Monthly Maximum Annual Pension Rate (Income Limit)**
Survivor (Death) Pension	$8,485 Medical expenses must exceed $424 to be deducted	$707 Medical expenses must exceed $35 to be deducted
One dependent child	$11,107	$926

Type of Benefit	**Maximum Annual Pension Rate (Income Limit)**	**Monthly Maximum Annual Pension Rate (Income Limit)**
Housebound (Survivor-Death Pension Rate)	$10,371	$864
One dependent child	$12,988	$1,082

Type of Benefit	**Maximum Annual Pension Rate (Income Limit)**	**Monthly Maximum Annual Pension Rate (Income Limit)**
Aid & Attendance (Survivor-Death Pension Rate)	$13,563	$1,130
One dependent child	$16,180	$1,348
Each add'l child	$2,161	+$180

About the Author

Attorney, Author, and Financial Advisor Wallace R. Nichols' practice consists of Estate Planning, VA Pension Planning, and Elder Law. The practice centers on wealth accumulation, asset protection, legacy planning, asset transfer strategies, and probate/fiduciary litigation. For over 20 years, Wally Nichols has successfully helped clients:

- develop wealth accumulation, protection and transfer strategies to ensure distribution of wealth in accord with clients' intentions;
- preserve their estates and legacies; and
- protect their rights against creditors and predators to the fullest extent of the law.

Wally began practicing law in 1992 engaged in general litigation, but concentrating in family law (high conflict resolution), probate litigation and debtor/creditor law. In 2011, Wally focused his practice on wealth accumulation and transfer strategies, legacy planning, business planning and succession strategies, all against the backdrop of asset protection. To provide clients the holistic funding solutions necessary to implement all of these strategies, Wally formed Asset Guidance Group, LLC in 2011, to allow him to provide clients financial services.

Financial Advisory Services

Asset Guidance Group

Since 2011, Wally has put his M.B.A. experience and legal knowledge to work for clients by providing financial advisory services through his company, Asset Guidance Group, LLC. Affiliated with an independent broker/dealer, Cetera Financial Networks LLC, Wally is backed up by an experienced staff of financial research analysts, strategic and tactical model portfolio allocations, third party money-managers, and the ability to create custom allocations for elite clients, to create and implement an optimal, suitable portfolio profile for every client. All accounts are housed with and protected by the security of custodian, Pershing, LLC, a BNY Mellon company. The result is that clients experience a litany of competent, peer-reviewed and forward-looking market assessments, professional investment advice, support, and service without the hassle of driving from office to office or the need to repeat their situation to multiple professionals. It's a powerful lineup and the best conservative approach!

Wally is a Member of WealthCounsel®, ElderCounsel®, national organizations of estate planning attorneys, is an accredited practitioner before the United States Department of Veterans Affairs, the National Association of Elder Law Attorneys, the
American Association for Justice, the National Association of Consumer Advocates, the 9th and 11th United States Circuit Courts of Appeal, the U.S. District Court of

Arizona, the U.S. Bankruptcy Court of the District of Arizona, the U.S. District Courts for the Northern and Middle Districts of Georgia and associated Bankruptcy Courts, and the District of Columbia.

Wally is also licensed by the States of Arizona and Georgia to sell Life, Variable and Indexed Annuities, Variable and Indexed Life products, and Health Insurance. Wally is recognized by the Financial Industry Regulatory Authority ("FINRA", formerly the National Association of Securities Dealers) as a qualified Broker and Investment Adviser. FINRA is the organization responsible for self-regulating securities industry participants, including stock brokers, brokerage firms, and exchanges such as NASDAQ. Wally is qualified to act as a General Securities Representative by successfully completing the FINRA required Series 7 and 66 examinations.

Wally has authored two books: Georgia Medicaid Planning 2012 and Pack a Sweater: Preparing Boomers for Long Term Care. Wally is a frequent public speaker and has taught continuing professional education classes for Georgia Social Workers and Attorneys.
You can contact Wally in his

Atlanta, Georgia office at 1532 Dunwoody Village Parkway Suite 205 in Atlanta, GA 30338 or at in Arizona by appointment only, at 8902 E Via Linda #110-155 Scottsdale, AZ 85258; 404-602-0040 or 480-478-0688.
http://wrnicholslaw.com;
http://assetguidancegroup.com;
http://atlantapersonalfamilylawyer.com;
http://atlantacreativebusinesslawyer.com.

Follow Wally on Twitter: @wrnicholslaw and @assetguidance; Also follow Wally on Facebook and LinkedIn and be sure to sign up for newsletters and updates!

Registered representative of, and advisory services offered through, Cetera Advisor Networks LLC, a Registered Investment Adviser, Member FINRA and SIPC. Cetera is under separate ownership from any other named entity.

ISBN 9780988295018 eBook
ISBN 9780988295025 Paperback